No. 126

Albert Cook Myers

THE BOY
George Washington
HIS ACCOUNT
OF AN INDIAN DANCE

THE BOY
George Washington
AGED 16
HIS OWN ACCOUNT OF AN
Iroquois Indian Dance
1748

BY

ALBERT COOK MYERS, 1874-1960

Chairman of The Historical Committee of *The Valley Forge Park Commission* and Secretary of *The Pennsylvania Historical Commission of* The Commonwealth of Pennsylvania

---

IN COMMEMORATION OF
THE TWO HUNDREDTH ANNIVERSARY OF
THE BIRTH OF GEORGE WASHINGTON
1732 - 1932

PHILADELPHIA:
Published by *Albert Cook Myers* at 1300 *Locust Street*
1932

970.1
Mye

PREFATORY NOTE

My thanks in particular are extended to Ernest Spofford, Librarian, and the other long suffering members of the staff of The Historical Society of Pennsylvania, and acknowledgments made to the works, supplementing original sources, of J. M. Toner, Moncure D. Conway, Worthington C. Ford, Lawrence C. Wroth, Charles Moore, John C. Fitzpatrick, Fairfax Harrison, Arthur C. Parker, and others. The three gentlemen last named, along with Donald A. Cadzow, George Morgan and Ellis Paxson Oberholtzer have kindly read the proof. I wish also to thank my sister, E. Mae Myers, and my nephew, J. Truman Underhill for their help.

ALBERT COOK MYERS

"Kentmere Lodge",
   Moylan, Delaware County,
   Pennsylvania.
   February 22, 1932.

George Washington's First Portrait, as a Virginia Colonel, in 1772, Aged 40.
Painted by Charles Willson Peale

ILLUSTRATIONS

THE BOY
George Washington
HIS ACCOUNT
OF AN INDIAN DANCE

A Journal of my Journey over
the Mountains begun ...
the 11th of March 17...

Fryday March 11th 17...
began my Journey in Compa
with George Fairfax Esqr, we tra
vell'd this day 40 Miles to Mr
George Neavels in Prince Willia
County

Saturday March 12th this Mor
ing Mr James Genn ye Surveyr
came to us we travell'd over ye Blue Ridge
to Capt Ashbys on Shannandoa
River, Nothing remarkable hap
pend

Sunday March 13 rode ...

First Page of Washington's First Journal, in his Own Hand, 1748. Size 3¾ x 6 Inches

THE BOY
𝕲𝖊𝖔𝖗𝖌𝖊 𝖂𝖆𝖘𝖍𝖎𝖓𝖌𝖙𝖔𝖓
HIS ACCOUNT OF AN INDIAN DANCE

THE boy George Washington got his first job, that of surveyor, and his initiation into wilderness life at the age of sixteen, in the year 1748. Of these experiences and his earliest backwoods journey on horseback from his Virginia home, on the lower Potomac, over the Blue Ridge Mountains into the frontier region of Western Maryland, on the borders of Pennsylvania, he has kept an interesting Journal. Written at that time, it is the first of the series of such records of his known to exist.

He entitles it: "A Journal of my Journey over | the Mountains. began Fryday | the 11th: of March 1747/8."[1] Covering a period of a little over a month, it ends April 13, 1748. The system of his dating, it must

---

[1] Leaf 40 verso.

be borne in mind, was according to the
Old Style, or Julian Calendar, the New
Style, or Gregorian system, with its ad-
dition of eleven days, not coming into use
until the year 1752. Although his birth
occurred February 11, Old Style, 1731–2,
yet it is celebrated, as all the World knows,
February 22, New Style.

The original manuscript of the Journal,
as preserved in the collection of Washington Papers in the Division of Manuscripts
of the Library of Congress, in the Capital
City of Washington, has been used in the
preparation of this little work. The Journal was written in a small pocket memo-
randum-book, of 42 leaves, of linen laid
paper, now tinted with age, in size 3¾x6
inches. In its original state the little book
was bound in vellum, but as a protection
from impious handling, it has been taken
apart and each leaf, covered with trans-
parent crêpeline, has been separately in-
laid on loose sheets of heavy paper (8¾x
11½ inches in size) to match. The old

riginal Old Vellum Cover of Washington's First Journal, 1748. Size 5⅞ x 7⅞ inches

vellum cover, too, time-stained and broken in parts, with one of its patina-coated brass clasps still firmly attached to the front has been set in a guard of heavy cardboard in uniformity with the sheets of the book and placed at its beginning. The whole is thus in readiness for rebinding.

The Journal occupies 25[1] pages of script, written on both sides of the leaves of the book, bearing the modern penciled numbers, 28 verso—40 verso. Only a few leaves are blank. The remainder of the book consists of surveying notes, drafts of letters, and like memoranda. Somewhat dim in parts, yet legible, all of the Journal and the other entries of the book are in George Washington's own handwriting, angular and less flowing and rounded than in his more mature years. In this Journal

---

[1] The last page is blank save for the four words of conclusion of the Journal at the top.

of 1748 young Washington has written his own account of the Iroquois Indian dance.

In its expert penmanship, its orthography, and its manner of expression, the Journal is, in a sense, an exemplification of George's personality, intelligence and early education. It is plain that he had a natural aptitude for mathematics, in particular becoming proficient in surveying. Epic in spirit, with its scenes and incidents so vividly pictured, the little book is a remarkable production for one so young, especially in view of his limited educational opportunities. All the evidence shows that the boy could apply himself to the task in hand.

Washington at this time of his relation was a comely youth, tall in stature, straight as an Indian, athletic and manly, with "one of the best of constitutions". Although broad shouldered, he was some-

George Washington, in 1779. Painted by Charles Willson Peale

what narrow-waisted and slender in appearance, but very muscular and strong, with long arms and unusually big hands and feet. His legs were long, large and sinewy, and his step elastic. His features were regular, his mouth large, his nose prominent, his forehead high, and his chin firm. His eyes were a light blue, rather large. His hair was a dark brown tied in a queue. His cheeks were smooth, as yet unmarked by the smallpox. His voice was agreeable rather than strong. His carriage was quietly forceful, but modest, with the deferential bearing of the gently bred of his class and period. He was a splendid horseman, and a true Virginian, he liked to talk about horses.

The eldest son of Augustine Washington (1694–1743), by the latter's second wife, Mary Ball (1708–1789), George Washington[1] (1732–1799) was born on one of the

---

[1] Of Washington's paternal and maternal ancestry see Appendix, page 65.

Washington estates, later called "Wake-field," on Bridges Creek, Westmoreland County, Virginia. At the time of entering his new employment he was a fatherless youth living higher up the Potomac, on another family estate, "Mount Vernon", with his married elder half-brother, Major Lawrence Washington (1718–1752), aged 30, who took the place of parent to his young brother. The latter ancestral plantation of the Washingtons, comprising 2500 acres, located in Fairfax County, Virginia, had descended to Lawrence from his father, Augustine Washington, his grandfather, Lawrence Washington (1659 –1697), and his great-grandfather, John Washington (c.1632–1677), the English immigrant forbear of the family.

Educated in England and far-travelled, Lawrence had served in the West Indies under Admiral Vernon, and on coming into his inheritance, he had changed the

Mount Vernon, Home of Washington. From the Etching by Arnold Anderson, 1922

name of the estate from its old Indian one
of Epsewasson, or Little Hunting Creek,
to Mount Vernon, in honor of his former
commander. He had been married, in 1743,
not long after the building of the new
mansion of "Mount Vernon", to Ann,
eldest daughter of his neighbor, William
Fairfax (1691–1757), of "Belvoir", a man
of culture and prominence in Virginia
affairs, sometime Acting Governor of the
Bahamas and Collector of Customs at
Salem, Massachusetts.

"Belvoir" was a beautiful seat, with a
large acreage, lying in the neck of land
immediately below "Mount Vernon". Although four miles apart, yet located as
they were on their respective promontories
of the west bank of the Potomac River,
the two mansions were almost in view of
each other over the water. This nearness
and relationship, as well as the quietude
of the region, brought the households into

a close intimacy, which included young George Washington.

The background of the boy in this impressionable, adolescent period had been confined to such refined and pleasant circles of the slaveholding aristocracy of the Tidewater. Now his horizon was to be widened by contact with the crude conditions of the upcountry Frontier. This change was brought about by the coming upon the scene of his first employer, who was destined still further greatly to influence George's character and career in his formative years.

This employer, famed in the history of Virginia and greatest of all the Colonial land magnates, was no less a personage than Lord Fairfax (Thomas Fairfax, 1693 –1781, the 6th Baron Fairfax of Cameron), head of a well-known Yorkshire county family seated at palatial Leeds Castle, County Kent, England, and possessing,

THOMAS, LORD FAIRFAX

besides his English estates, a vast American domain of over 5,000,000 acres, known as the Northern Neck of Virginia.

Educated at Oriel College, Oxford University, sometime Treasurer of the Royal Household, this nobleman, a bachelor of 54, arrived a second time in Virginia, in the early summer of 1747, there to spend the remainder of his days in the development of his Proprietary of the Northern Neck. This princely tract of land, which he had inherited through his mother, from her father, Lord Culpeper (Thomas, Baron Culpeper of Thoresway, 1635–1689, Governor of Virginia, 1675–1682), embraced the northern part of Virginia, between the Potomac and the Rappahannock Rivers, extending from the Chesapeake Bay to the headwaters of the Potomac. At first Lord Fairfax came to stay for a few years with his cousin and agent for his Virginia estates, William Fairfax, at "Belvoir", where his land office was located, but some years later he made his final home at "Greenway Court", in the Valley of Virginia.

Here it was, then, at "Belvoir", that same summer of 1747, that his Lordship learned to know young George Washington, forming such a good opinion of the boy and his unusual abilities that he engaged George to join the surveying expedition he was sending, early in the coming year of 1748, to measure some of his lands over the mountains in the Valley.

The leadership of the expedition was committed to William Fairfax's able son, George William Fairfax (1725–1787), a single young man of 23, educated in England, who previously had been on surveying trips over the mountains and who was to succeed his father in the agency of his Lordship's estates. In spite of the eight years' difference in their ages, the two

Georges were close friends and congenial companions. With the ardent expectation of their young years they set forth on their journey of work and adventure.

From "Belvoir", "Fryday March 11th: 1747/8" (Old Style), the young scribe records, "Began my Journey in Compa[ny] with George Fairfax, Esqr.; we travell'd this day 40 Miles to M^r. George Neavels [inn] in Prince Willia[m] County [now the village of Auburn, in Fauquier County]."[1] The next day, being joined by James Genn, County Surveyor of Prince William County, the young horsemen rode further up into the Piedmont region, over the Blue Ridge through Ashby's Gap, into the Valley of Virginia.

The surveyors "travled over Hills and Mountains"[2] and had now come to the region assigned by his Lordship for meas-

---

[1] Leaf 40 verso.
[2] Leaf 29 verso.

urement. Beginning with that part of it known as the Shenandoah Valley, with the help of chainmen and like assistants, for the next few weeks the task went busily forward. The wet springtime and consequently swollen streams were the only delays. Not a little of the Journal is given to particulars as to surveys. In the Valley "We went throug[h] most beautiful Groves of Sugar Trees", George notes, "& spent y. best part of y. Day in admiring y. Trees & richness of y. Land"; "produces abundance of Grain Hemp Tobacco[1] &c". Only one "Rattled Snake"[2] was seen. Some wild turkeys were shot. But an unlucky day for such game was, "Fryday April y. 1st 1748 This Morning Shot twice at Wild Turkies but killed none run of[f] three Lots & returned to Camp"[3]

[1] Leaf 40.
[2] Leaf 29.
[3] Leaf 34.

Washington "calld to see y. Fam'd Warm Springs,"[1] at what is now Bath, or Berkeley Springs, in Morgan County, West Virginia.

On the fifth day of the trip, Tuesday, the 15th, begins a series of entries indicating how George was missing the refinements of his Tidewater home as he depicts in his valuable record some of the primitive ways of the backwoods country:

"Worked hard till Night and then return'd to" Captain Isaac Pennington's, 16 miles below present Winchester. "We got our Suppers and I was Lighted into a Room & I not being so good a Woodsman as y. rest of my Company striped my self very orderly & went in to y. Bed as they called it when to my Surprize I found it to be nothing but a Little Straw Matted together without Sheets or any thing else but only one thread Bear blanket with double its

---

[1] Leaf 37 verso.

Weight of Vermin such as Lice Fleas[1]
&c I was glad to get up (as soon as y.
Light was carried from us) I put on my
Cloths and Lay as my Companions Had
we not been very tired I am sure we should
not have slep'd much that night I made a
Promise not to Sleep so from that time
forward chusing rather to sleep in y. open
Air before a fire."[2]

The following day, Wednesday, the
16th, having come to Frederick Town,
now Winchester "where our Baggage came
to us we cleaned ourselves (to get Rid of
y. Game we had catched y^e. Night before)
& took a Review of y. Town & then return'd to our Lodgings where we had a
good Dinner prepar'd for us Wine & Rum
Punch in Plenty & a good Feather Bed

---

[1] "Kill no Vermin as Fleas, lice ticks &c in the Sight of
Others", is one of the long list of "Rules of Civility", copied
by him in his own hand, in 1745.

[2] Leaves 39 verso—39.

Wednesday 16th. We set out early
by & finish'd about one oClock &
then Travelled up to Frederick Town
where our Baggage came to us we
cleaned ^ourselves^ & to get red of ye Game we
had catched ~~the~~ ye Night be-
fore) & took a Review of ye Town & then
returnd to our Lodgings where we
had a good Dinner prepar'd for us
Wine & Rum Punch in Plenty & a
good Feather Bed with clean Sheets
which was a very agreeable re-
gule.

with clean Sheets which was a very agree-able regale".[1]

At another house, he writes, that of "Solomon Hedges Esqr one of his Majestys Justices of ye Peace for ye. County of Frederick where we camped when we came to Supper there was neither a Cloth upon ye Table nor a Knife to eat with but as good luck would have it we had Knives of [our] own."[2]

Once when they were surveying certain lands, he states, there came "a great Company of People Men Women & Children that attended us through ye. Woods as we went shewing their Antick tricks I really think they seem to be as Ignorant a Set of People as the Indians they would never speak English but when spoken to they speak all Dutch [i.e. German]".[3]

---

[1] Leaf 38 verso.
[2] Leaf 35.
[3] Leaves 33—32 verso.

Of his mountain travel and camping out is this description:

"Fryday [April] 8th. we breakfasted at Casseys & Rode down to Vanmetris's to get all our Company together which when we had accomplished we Rode down below y^e. Trough in order to Lay of[f] Lots there we laid of[f] one this day The Trough is a couple of Ledges of Mountain Impassable running side & Side together for above 7 or 8 Miles & y^e. River down between them you must Ride Round y^e. back of y^e. Mountain for to get below them we Camped this Night in y^e. Woods near a Wild Meadow where was a Large Stack of Hay after we had Pitched our Tent & made a very Large Fire we pull'd out our Knap Sack in order to Recruit ourselves every [one] was his own Cook our Spits was Forked Sticks our Plates was a Large Chip as for Dishes we had none"[1]

---

[1] Leaves 31—30 verso.

On another "blowing & Rainy night Our Straw catch'd a Fire yᵗ we were laying upon & was luckily Preserv'd by one of our Mens awaking when it was in a [blaze]"[1]

In a letter, contemporary with the foregoing Journal extracts, he informs a friend that he is "amongst a parcel of Barbarians and an uncooth set of People. ... I have not sleep'd above three Nights or four in a bed but after Walking a good deal all the Day lay down before the fire upon a Little Hay Straw Fodder or bairskin whichever is to be had with Man Wife and Children like a Parcel of Dogs or Catts & happy's he that gets the Birth nearest the fire ... I have never had my Cloths of[f] but lay and sleep in them like a Negro except the few Nights I have lay'n in Frederick Town".[2]

---

[1] Leaf 33 verso.
[2] Leaves 17 verso—18.

On Monday, March 21st a diversion of
a few days from the surveying labors of
the party began, a short excursion being
made over into Maryland, which they
reached by swimming their horses through
the high waters of the Potomac and themselves crossing in a canoe. Journeying up
the River "all ye Day," George writes,
"in a Continued Rain" over "I believe y.
worst Road that ever was trod by Man or
Beast."[1]

At nightfall they arrived at the hos-
pitable abode of Maryland's vanguard
pioneer, Colonel Thomas Cresap (1703–
1790), an Englishman, from Skipton, in
Yorkshire, whose stockaded house and
trading post was at what is now Oldtown,
Allegany County.

A more than ordinary human interest
attaches to this man, for several days
host of the youth who was to be one of

---

[1] Leaf 37.

the great ones of the earth. A particular account, therefore, follows, at somewhat disproportionate length, of Cresap and his background, more especially of his Iroquois visitors and his relations with them. This precedes, in a supplementary way, young Washington's all too brief recital concerning these redmen.

Indian trader, trail blazer, road maker, farmer, cattleman, and general promoter, Cresap was a picturesque character, known far and wide by redman and white man. Virile, rough-spoken, aged 45, he was a leader in the conquest of the wilderness, of a rugged frontier type, in sharp contrast to the young Journalist's employer, the restrained and cultivated aristocrat, Thomas, Lord Fairfax, Baron of Cameron.

Now, be it known, that while Colonel Cresap thus appears as a glamourous frontier figure in the annals of Western

Maryland, yet a dozen years earlier, in his younger manhood, he had an ill reputation over the line in the Province of Pennsylvania, whither, in 1730, he had removed from the neighborhood of present Havre de Grace, Maryland, and under a title from the latter Province had made a buffer settlement in the territory on the west side of the Susquehanna River, then in dispute between Lord Baltimore (Charles Calvert, 1699–1751, 5th Baron Baltimore), Proprietor of Maryland, and the Penn Proprietors of Pennsylvania. Cresap's grant of land was taken out of the old Indian lands of Conejohela, on the Susquehanna, at present Long Level, 18 miles north of the later Mason and Dixon Line and three miles south of what is now Wrightsville, on the Lincoln Highway, in York County. The main part of the grant, extending to the bank of the River, he named "Pleasant Gardens," while the

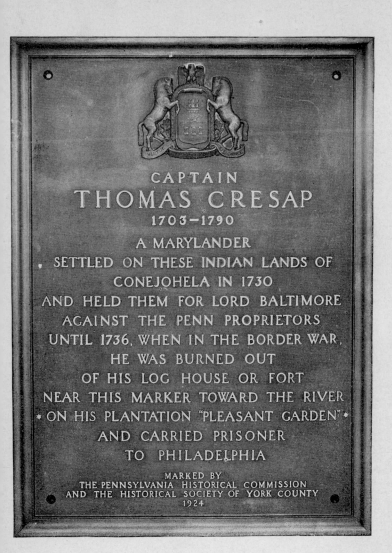

CAPTAIN
THOMAS CRESAP
1703–1790

A MARYLANDER
, SETTLED ON THESE INDIAN LANDS OF
CONEJOHELA IN 1730
AND HELD THEM FOR LORD BALTIMORE
AGAINST THE PENN PROPRIETORS
UNTIL 1736, WHEN IN THE BORDER WAR,
HE WAS BURNED OUT
OF HIS LOG HOUSE OR FORT
NEAR THIS MARKER TOWARD THE RIVER
* ON HIS PLANTATION "PLEASANT GARDEN" *
AND CARRIED PRISONER
TO PHILADELPHIA

MARKED BY
THE PENNSYLVANIA HISTORICAL COMMISSION
AND THE HISTORICAL SOCIETY OF YORK COUNTY
1924

Thomas Cresap Marker Tablet

Thomas Cresap Marker on Susquehanna River, York County, Pennsylvania

adjacent islands, also within his claim, he called "Isles of Promise."[1]

Here he had held sway for six years, the aggressive, ruffian leader of the murderous border warfare that was carried on, but all in vain was his attempt to hold the region for his noble patron; in 1736, under the authority of the Penns,[2] he was besieged in his log house or fort, burned out of it, and carried prisoner to Philadelphia. Upon his first glimpse of the little city of that day upon the banks of the Delaware, which he regarded as within the northern boundary of Maryland, the mildest of the "horrid Oaths & Imprecations" and revilings of which he relieved himself was:

---

[1] After his enforced departure Cresap sold these properties to John Myers, son of Jacob Myers, from the Lancaster County side of Susquehanna River, this title later being confirmed by the Penn Proprietors.

[2] Proprietor Thomas Penn (1702–1775), son of William Penn (1644–1718), the Founder, being then in Pennsylvania, was the directing spirit in the suppression of Cresap.

"Damn it ... this is one of the Prettyest Towns in Maryland"!

Although thus a failure, these years before, in his mission for Lord Baltimore in Pennsylvania, yet Cresap had attained a great success, as stated above, in the constructive work of the development of his Lordship's own Province, as early as 1740, having become the westernmost settler of Maryland here at the abandoned Indian village site of the Shawnee Old Town (Chief Opessa's Town) on Potomac River, opposite the mouth of its South Branch.

This choice of location had been a strategic one; it was not only a stage in westward journeys from Virginia, Maryland and Pennsylvania, but also a station on the old Indian trail customarily taken by the Iroquois of New York on their expeditions against the Cherokees and Catawbas on the Carolina frontier. Canoeing down the Susquehanna to the Indian settlements in Pennsylvania, to Paxton Indian Town (present Harrisburg) and, in the earlier period, as far as to a point near Conestoga Indian Town (present Lancaster County), these warriors followed the southern path, which the whites in treaties, from time to time, with the progress of the frontier, succeeded in moving farther to the west.

Cresap is said to have kept a big kettle suspended ready to kindle a fire under, near a spring, for the use of the Indians as they came by his place. For this reason they called him the "Big Spoon."

Who were these Iroquois Indians, the first of the many aborigines young Washington was to meet, and with whom he was to be for a day and a half here at Cresap's in the backwoods of Maryland?

The early white settlers of the Atlantic seaboard of North America encountered two great family groups of rival Indians, the Iroquoian and the Algonquian, each comprising many tribes.

The Iroquois, so called by the French, formed a powerful confederacy,—said to date from about the year 1570—of the Mohawks, Oneidas, Onondagas, Cayugas, Senecas, and lastly, in the year 1723, of the Tuscaroras. By the English they were named the Five Nations, until the admission of the Tuscaroras; thereafter they were known as the Six Nations.

The habitat of the Iroquois was largely in the present State of New York, east and south of Lakes Erie and Ontario. This area, while offering fewer physical obstacles and greater exposure to enemy attack than the natural defenses of the Appalachian barriers and similar physiographic advantages of the regions to the south and north, was strategically, nevertheless, the commanding thoroughfare from the interior to the seaboard. Notwithstanding these disadvantages of physical geography the Iroquois were able to intrench themselves and present an impenetrable bulwark of defense against attacks, exercising a sort of feudal sway over a large territory, occupied by many tribes.

Disposed to a sedentary and agricultural life and skilled in the art of fortification and housebuilding, they dwelt in palisaded villages, including communal long houses, often 80 to 100 feet in length. Onondaga was the capital town, where their great council was held. This was re-located, in 1720, a few miles south of Onondaga Lake and the present city of Syracuse.

In political organization, statecraft and military prowess the Iroquois were foremost among the North American Indians. Their leaders were astute diplomats, often proving more than a match for the white invaders. The most warlike natives of the eastern North Atlantic, they were ever in conflict with neighboring Indians, particularly the Algonquians.

The coming to New France of its picturesque leader, Samuel de Champlain (c. 1567–1635), and his making common cause with the Algonquians in defeating the Iroquois in 1609, turned the latter into implacable enemies of the French and indispensable allies of the Dutch and, of their successors, the English.

In spite of the many attempts by French missionaries and traders to break the English alliance, the Iroquois remained firm in this friendship until the close of the French regime in 1763, in fact until the end of their power. This loyalty, however, was due not so much to the ancient enmity towards the French as to favorable economic factors: (1) the profitable traffic in beaver skins, which the Iroquois in their dominating natural location, as middlemen, drew from the hinterland Indians and disposed of more advantageously to the English, the English giving more and better merchandise for peltries than the French; (2) the large amounts of money and goods these Indians were able to exact by treaty from the English, especially from Pennsylvania, Maryland, and Virginia, in payment of back country land claims acquired from conquered Indians.

The League of the Iroquois thus became an effective buffer for the westward expanding English settlements against French aggression. This barrier, however, had to be reinforced from time to time by the English, often by inter-colonial action, although, for a long time, under the leadership or mediation of the governors of New York. Albany, in the early periods, was the place of treaty, as well as the center of the Indian trade.

Such strength did the Iroquois attain that in time they almost exterminated the ancient Susquehannas or Minquas Indians (of Iroquoian stock), in the lower Susquehanna River Valley of present Pennsylvania, and became finally the overlords of the Delawares, or Lenni Lenape, and indeed of nearly all the neighboring Algonquian tribes.

It was in quest of more worlds to conquer, long before the settlement of Pennsylvania, that the Iroquois had extended their war-paths southward in enforcement of their claim of suzerainty over the Cherokee (of Iroquoian stock), and the Catawbas (of Siouian stock) on the Carolina frontier. Although of a milder disposition, yet these southern Indians continued to resist the periodic incursions of the ambitious young warriors of the northern enemy. Thus through many years the feud was prolonged.

Now, these same young marauders in their passage through the upcountry and hinterland valleys of Virginia and Maryland,—a land they claimed as hunting territory by right of conquest of the local Indians—were ever ravaging the white pioneers in the progressive advance of the frontier of settlement of those regions.

This made a difficult problem for the Chesapeake Colonies. They had to move cautiously. They must not offend such important allies. The wily Iroquois well knew that they held the balance of power between the English and the French and took every advantage of it. The excuse made by the older Iroquois for the depredations of their young men was that they could not restrain the ardor of youth on the war-path so far away.

In the endeavor to settle these troubles several successive treaties with the Iroquois were made at Albany, with varying success. In 1677, such a mission was headed by Henry Coursey, of Maryland,

in behalf of Maryland and Virginia; in
1679, by William Kendall, of Virginia;
and again, in 1682, by Coursey.

But the most notable of these early
compacts was made in 1684, by Thomas
Dongan (1634–1720; the 2nd Earl of
Limerick, 1698), Governor of New York,
1682–1691, in conjunction with Lord
Howard of Effingham (Francis Howard,
1643–1726; the 5th Baron Howard of
Effingham), Governor of Virginia, 1683–
1693, in which the Indians acknowledged
themselves subjects of England and agreed
to move their southern war-path to the
eastern foot of the Blue Ridge Mountains.

At the Albany Treaty of 1722, in which
William Burnet (1688–1729), Governor of
New York, 1720–1728, and Sir William
Keith, Baronet (1680–1749), Governor of
Pennsylvania, 1717–1726, participated,
Alexander Spotswood (1676–1740), Gover-
nor of Virginia, 1710–1722, quieted the

Indian title of the piedmont in his province and transferred the war-path over the Blue Ridge to the Valley of Virginia. On that occasion he gave the Indians one of his famous golden horseshoes to be worn as a token of friendship when they should come on their travels southward.

Pennsylvania had now become more directly a link in the chain of the Iroquois relations, particularly about a decade after the passing of William Penn (1644–1718), when the Iroquois, having completed their control of the Delawares, succeeded to certain of the land claims of their subjects in that Province, as yet not extinguished by the Penn Proprietors. Previously the great Founder's land dealings had been with the Delawares alone; although the Iroquois had appeared in a minor way at a few of his conferences with the red men.

Well aware of their key position on the continent and aroused to the material possibilities of these land claims, as the white settlers came increasingly into the back country, the acquisitive conquerors, with much adroitness, pressed their claims upon the Pennsylvania authorities.

Following the earlier negotiations at Conestoga in Governor Keith's time,— in one of which, in 1721, he sent to the head Iroquois chief a gold coronation medal of King George I—, a series of important treaties with the Iroquois took place at Philadelphia, in 1732, 1736 and 1742. Leading chieftains, well attended, came the long journey from New York and with the usual picturesque ceremonial kept the Chain of Friendship brightened, for their own benefit, to the extent of many hundreds of pounds, as they released the respective land claims.

Pennsylvania proving such a fruitful field, a similar profitable yield was sought from Maryland and Virginia in the further

quieting of the tributary Indian claims in
those provinces. With renewed skirmishes
in the Valley of Virginia and other artful
manoeuverings, an even greater conference, with these colonies as the chief par-
ticipants, in due course, was arranged for,
Pennsylvania becoming the mediator.
This was the great Treaty of Lancaster,
of 1744.

Of the agents in the preliminaries for
this outstanding Indian conference of the
period, as in those immediately mentioned
above, the Iroquois intermediary was
Shikellamy (died 1748), an Oneida chief,
who, as early as 1728, had been sent by
the Onondaga Council to the forks of the
Susquehanna in Pennsylvania to guard
the Iroquois interests in that Province
and to have general oversight of the tributary Delawares there and of the near by
Shawanese. This point on the east bank
of the River to which this shrewd and

capable chieftain came was Shamokin Indian Town (present Sunbury), the capital of the head chief of the Delawares, Sassoonan or Allumapees (died 1747), who stated that as a boy he had witnessed the landing of William Penn.

The mediator for the whites and the director of the Treaty arrangements, under Governor Thomas, was the famous Indian interpreter and diplomat, Conrad Weiser (1696–1760), a native German, living in the Tulpehocken Valley, near present Womelsdorf, in Berks County, Pennsylvania. As a boy in New York Colony he had become an adopted Mohawk and thus was familiar with the habits, customs, and language of those Indians.

Of the highest personal character, efficient and long experienced, Weiser retained the confidence of both the Iroquois and the white men, and under the guidance of

James Logan (1674–1751), the faithful and able representative of the Penn Proprietors, was for a long period the guardian of the Indian policy of Pennsylvania. He and Shikellamy became close friends.

Thomas Cresap himself, by the appointment of Thomas Bladen[1] (1698–1780), Governor of Maryland, 1742–1746, had made a strong effort to induce the Iroquois to hold the Treaty at his house in Maryland,[2] but he was given no part in the negotiations. Apart from the disfavor in which he was still held in Pennsylvania,

---

[1] His manuscript letter of March 24, 1743–4, to the Six Nations.—Peters Papers, II. 6 (Historical Society of Pennsylvania).

[2] See Cresap's holograph letter, dated "Antedem", April 2, 1743, addressed to "Shecalama at Shehemokie Near Susquhana River".—*Ibid.*, I., 118; letter of William Gooch (1681–1751), Governor of Virginia, 1727–1749, dated January 11, 1743–4, to Governor Thomas of Pennsylvania.—*Ibid.*, II., 1; letter of George Thomas (c. 1705–1775), Governor of Pennsylvania, 1738–1747, dated Philadelphia, January 20, 1743–4, to Governor Gooch of Virginia.—*Ibid.*, II., 2; letter of Levin Gale, Annapolis, July 7, 1743, to Conrad Weiser.—*Ibid.*, I., 121.

Conrad Weiser reports, in the spring of 1744, that Cresap is not "in any favour with the Said [Iroquois] Indians at all ... they look upon him as a man that Either wants Wit or Honesty because for his Ill management last Sumer in Endeavouring to buy land of the [Iroquois] Warriours."[1] Lancaster, besides, was found to be a place with better accommodations.

The Lancaster Treaty of 1744, one of the most colorful and significant of the colonial Indian conferences, lasting almost two weeks, is vividly chronicled by Witham Marshe, the young clerk of the Maryland Commissioners.

It was late in June that the delegations reached this little backwoods Pennsylvania town. Governor Thomas, of Pennsylvania, the presiding officer, and the Commissioners of Virginia and Maryland were the first to arrive. They awaited the com-

---

[1] *Ibid.*, II., 5.

ing of the Indians in the court-house, where the ceremonies took place.

Hither, under conduct of Conrad Weiser, came the motley procession of the Iroquois, over 250 of them, chiefs, warriors, squaws, and children, some of the latter on horseback. At their head marched the highest of the Iroquois chiefs, Canassatego (died 1750), the noted Onondaga sachem, then about sixty years old, famed as an orator, tall, full-chested, brawny-limbed, and of a manly, good-natured countenance. As he approached the court-house this chief, writes Marshe, sang "in the Indian language a song, inviting us to a renewal of all treaties heretofore made, and that now to be made". The Indian party then withdrew to the outskirts of the town, where they rested for a few days from their wearisome journey in the wigwams they erected.

The second day of their coming, June 23rd, the Indians were visited by Marshe, who thus interestingly writes of them and their dancing:

"After supper, this evening, I went with Mr. President [James] Logan's son,[1] and divers other young gentlemen, to the Indian's camp, they being then dancing one of their lighter war dances.

"They performed it after this manner: Thirty or forty of the younger men formed themselves into a ring, a fire being lighted (notwithstanding the excessive heat) and burning clear in the midst of them. Near this, sat three elderly Indians, who beat a drum to the time of the others' dancing. Then the dancers hopped round the ring, after a frantic fashion, not unlike the priests of Bacchus in old times, and repeated, sundry times, these sounds, *Yohoh!*

---

[1] William Logan (1718–1776).

Bugh! Soon after this, the major part of the dancers (or rather hoppers) set up a horrid shriek or halloo!

"They continued dancing and hopping, after this manner, several hours, and rested very seldom. Once, whilst I staid with them, they did rest themselves; immediately thereupon, the three old men began to sing an Indian song, the tune of which was not disagreeable to the white by-standers. Upon this, the young warriors renewed their terrible shriek and halloo, and formed themselves into a ring, environing the three old ones, and danced as before.

"Sat up till eleven o'clock ... I heard the Indian drum, and the warriors repeating their terrible noise and dancing; and at this sport of theirs, they continued till near one in the morning. These young men are surprisingly agile, strong, and straight limbed. They shoot, both with

the gun and bow and arrow, most dexter-
ously. They likewise throw their toma-
hawk (or little hatchet) with great cer-
tainty, at an indifferent large object, for
twenty or thirty yards distance. This
weapon they use against their enemies,
when they have spent their powder and
ball, and destroy many of them with it."
The next day, Sunday, June 24, continues
Marshe:

"In the evening, walked to the Indian
camp, where they were dancing in the
manner described last night, only the
number of dancers was augmented, they
having taken in several small boys to
make a larger ring."

On a later evening Marshe accompanied
a friend "to the Indian cabins, where,
having collected several of their papooses
(or little children) together, he flung a
handful of English half-pennies amongst
them, for which they scrambled heartily,

and with the utmost earnestness. This pleased the elder sort very much; and they esteem it a great mark of friendship, if the white people make presents to their children, or treat them with particular notice. I gave the papooses some small beads, which were kindly received."

The Treaty proper began June 25th and ended July 4th, with frequent mutual expressions of good will and renewals of friendship and drinking of toasts. The proceedings, which comprise thirty-nine closely printed octavo pages of the official report,[1] include long speeches, arguments and detailed historical recitals. The Indians presented their side of the case in their customary, picturesque, figurative language, displaying much eloquence and ability; Conrad Weiser was the interpreter. Each important statement of the re-

---

[1] *The Minutes of the Provincial Council of Pennsylvania, IV.* (Harrisburg, Penn'a, 1851), pages 698–737.

spective sides was emphasized by the gift of strings and belts of wampum, accompanied by a cry of approbation from the Indians. This utterance was usual, states Marshe, "on presenting wampum to the Indians in a treaty, and is performed thus: The grand chief and speaker amongst them pronounces the word *jo-hah!*[1] with a loud voice, singly; then all the others join in this sound, *woh!* dwelling some little while upon it, and keeping exact time with each other, and immediately, with a sharp noise and force, utter this sound, *wugh!* This is performed in good order, and with the utmost ceremony and decorum; and with the Indians is like our English huzza!"

On the 30th, a great dinner, with much toasting and exchanging of compliments,

----

[1] " 'Jo-hah', a loud shout or cry of approbation, of a few notes by all the Indians in a very musical manner."—*Minutes of the Provincial Council of Pennsylvania, IV.* (Harrisburg, Penn'a, 1851) 701.

was given by Governor Thomas, and the Commissioners to twenty-four of the chiefs, who, says Marshe, "seemed prodigiously pleased with the feast, for they fed lustily, drank heartily, and were very greasy before they finished, ... for they made no use of forks."

Later that day, the Marylanders, having "put about the glass pretty briskly", induced the Indians to sign a deed of release for the back lands of Maryland, on terms that seemed mutually satisfactory, the payment being over £200 in goods and £100 in gold, and one of the chiefs receiving a broad, gold-laced hat. On this same occasion a head chief with much eloquence gave to the Governor of Maryland the Indian name of Tocarryhogan, meaning excellency.

July 2nd, the Indians signed a deed for the back lands of Virginia, in consideration of £200 in goods and £200 in gold, having previously stipulated that they were to have the use of the Waggon Road through the Valley of Virginia for their traveling bands and "reasonable Victuals when we are in want"; to Canassatego was given a scarlet coat.

At the same time, Governor Thomas in behalf of the Province of Pennsylvania gave the Indians £300 worth of goods. In return the Indians assured the three governments of their resolution to hinder the French from making any attempts against the English.

After the signing of the deed this day, writes Marshe, "Cannasatego commanded the young Indian men, then present, to entertain the Governor and commissioners, in the evening, with a particular dance, according to the custom of their nation; which was complied with about 8 o'clock. Before they performed the dance, I went to their camp, where I saw the young warriors paint themselves in a frightful manner, and on their heads place a great quantity of feathers. They took arrows and tomahawks in their hands, and then unanimously ran out of their camp, hallooing and shrieking (which was terrible to us, being strangers) up the street to Mr. [Thomas] Cookson's, where the Governor was; and there they made a ring, a person being placed in it, and danced round him to a horrid noise, made by the inclosed person, and the others. In this manner they continued some time, flourishing their weapons, and striving to destroy him in the ring. When they had acted thus about seven or eight minutes, then their captain ran before them, very swift, to another place ... This was a representation of the Indians besieging a fort of their enemies, (who have no cannon) the person in the midst of the circle representing the fort besieged, and

the Indians encircling them, the be-
sigers", etc.

At the close of the Treaty, having been
informed that the English had defeated
the French, Canassatego remarked that
much rum must have been captured and
that some of it could now well be spared
to let the Indians join in the rejoicing. At
which hint a dram for each of those present was given in a small glass called a
"French glass". Thereupon, Canassatego
said that he preferred the good sized
"English glass". As this second hint, to
the cry of five *jo-hahs*, was carried out,
Governor Thomas, with quick wit, responded that he was glad the chief dis-
liked what was French, for "They cheat
you in your Glasses as well as in every-
thing else."

The differences being settled and peace
renewed, the Indians departed well satisfied with the hospitality and the large
remuneration accorded them.

But in spite of the Treaty, the traveling bands of the young Iroquois were still difficult to deal with, as thus reported to the Assembly of Maryland, in the early summer of 1748, when Cresap vainly requested of that body reimbursement for his expenditures on account of such a party of Indians:

"Their Warriors cannot Possibly carry any Provisions with them nor Subsist without it and if they cannot get the Necessarys of Life without Violence, will take it, which of Course will create such Difference between them, and those from whom they forceably take what they want, as may very Probably end in Blood Shed and Slaughter; The Indians March in Parties and have Armes in their hands, which make them a Great Over Match for our Back Inhabitants who Live remote from one another and are in a Defenceless Condition, which must Expose them to the Rage & fury of the former, and were Our People ever so inclinable for their own Safety to supply the Indians, they are not able to do it to their Satisfaction and doing it Partially would not Secure them, and the Dissatisfaction of the Indians may Probably involve this Province in an Indian War; as this is our Case it Certainly Deserves the attention of the Legislature, and it is Good Policy to avert the Danger as it may be done at a trifling Expence by furnishing Provision and some other Necessaries at the Publick Charge for the Indians in going to and Returning from the southward".

Again, a year later, Cresap vividly recites his further troubles with the Indians and seeks financial redress, in the following letter, addressed to the Governor of Maryland and transmitted to the Assembly of that Province:

"To his Excellency Samuel Ogle, Esq:
Maryland.

May it please your Excellency, ...

I have had sundry Companies of Indian Warriors passing and repassing, some of which have been very insolent and saucy; in particular, a Company of about 44, who had three Women and two Boy Prisoners with them, taken from the Catawbees, while the Men were out hunting. ...

"These Indians stayed at my House four Days, and complained of Hunger; I gave them at their first coming two Bushels of Meal, and one Bushel of Corn; and as it was bad Weather, I took the three Captains in my House to lodge; they being very naked for Cloaths, complained that they had lost their Cloaths and Guns almost all in Fight; and one of the Captains told me, that he was Conasadago's Brother, who was the Speaker at the Treaty

of Lancaster [in Pennsylvania, in 1744].
They held several Councils here, and told
me that I was their Brother, and that they
had given me this Land, and that they
had no Powder or Lead to carry them
home: but that I must give them Powder
and Lead and Knives and Flints and
Stockings and Tommyhawks, and mend
their Kettles and Guns; on which I gave
them 20 lb. Weight of Powder, and some
Lead; but they not being satisfied, called
another Council, and wanted more Victuals; I gave them two Flitches of Bacon,
and four Bushels of Meal; they complain-
ing they wanted on the road, and in Hopes
of being rid of them; but stayed and eat
up the Victuals given them. They then
called a third Council, and wanted me to
give them a Cow, which I told them I
could not do; at which they began to be
mad, and told me I was no good: On
which I told them, if they wanted to fight

to let me know, for if they killed my Cow I would kill them; and so quitted their Council, and loaded my Guns, expecting to have had a Fight: They went to their Cabin, loaded their Guns, and fired off several, and ran about shouting and whooping all Night. Next Morning I found several of my Hogs shot with Arrows; they stole sundry things, and went off. ...

"The Burden is so great on me in supporting these Indians, that my Patience is quite tired out; so that if the Government will not allow me something towards the Expence, I must, tho' contrary to my Inclination, of Necessity enter into a Quarrel with them, at the Risque of my own Life, and Family's also; which may cost the Government more than allowing them 30 or 40 l. per Year, or perhaps less, for three or four Years to come; and it may in that Time be over. ... I am, in all Respects,

Your Excellency's most humble Servant,
                    Thomas Cresap
March 17, 1749–50."

As before, the Assembly would not
undertake "any Charge on Account of
those Indians, who if encouraged, would
always find Persons to set them to Work,
either for private Interest or some other
Views."

Finally, one of these Indian parties
took such liberties with Cresap's property,
that he was exasperated to desperation.
The affair threatened to become so serious
that Governor Ogle, in 1751, gave a detailed account of it to the Assembly. Eye
witnesses stated in this report that "a
Company of Indian Warriors of the Six
Nations," "Consisting of fifty," under
"four Captains", came to Colonel Cresap's
and "Campt in said Cresaps Pasture."
"They killed several of his Hogs, took his
Corn Flour and Bread", and "killed a

Beef," "which made the said Cresap fall
into a Passion & threaten to Load his
Guns and Shoot among them at Night,"
"when they were Dancing a War dance."
But the noted frontiersman, Christopher
Gist (c.1706–1759) at a later time, twice
the savior of Washington's life, and other
white traders being present, "prevailed
with" Cresap "not to Shoot," at the same
time urging upon the Indians "the Hardships Thomas Cresap Suffered by their
killing his Creatures." To this the head
Indian Captain responded that there was
no hardship on Cresap's part, "for their
Brother Togerahogan" (i.e. Governor
Ogle) "Paid Cresap for all the Provisions
they destroyed at his House." Cresap
"affirmed" that this "was false, that he
never was Paid."

Thereupon, "as there was one of the
Traders that could speak their Tongue
very well" the Indians were desired to

present their case to Governor Ogle;
"upon which [the] four Captains made"
the following "Speech" to him, as "Witt-
ness Our hands Septem^r 14th 1751

 James Martin   Christ Gist
   his
John M. Miller   Michael Aldridge:
   mark
"Brother Tograhogan

We are Sorry to find that we are under
this Necessity of making this Complaint
to you which has happened at a Time
when we met a proper Person to be an
Interpreter between us and our brother
Cresap who has of late Seemed angry with
us and we did not know for what and find-
ing he did not give us Victuals so chear-
fully as usual our Young men went out
and killed Sundry of his Hogs at which he
flew into a Passion with us and had it not
happened that there was a Proper Interpreter who told us that our Brother To-

grahogan did not Pay for the Victuals which they took and was Promised to be given us at the Treaty of Lancaster on our Travels to and from War therefore we refer you to the Treaty, and as the White People has killed up the Deer, Buffalos, Elks & Bears there is nothing for us to live on but what we get from the White people and having no White People on the Road from Onondago to Our Brother Cresaps house we are often very hungry and Stays three or four days to Rest ourselves and Our Young men very unruly goes into the Woods and kills Our Brother Cresaps Hogs & Sometimes Cattle Therefore We recommend this to you in hopes you will do us Justice and Provide for us according to the Treaty, which will prevent any differences that may arise between us & Your People.

"If any of your People hurts any of us we shall look upon it as if done by you. This

we Speak now in Publick before our friend
Christopher Gist and Several Indian
Traders, Who puts their Marks in this
Paper to Testify We have told you all
this

	his			his	
Henry	X		Musk	X	Ratt
	mark			mark	
	his			his	
Barley	X		The	X	Ground
	mark			mark"	

The Assembly, however, remained ob-
durate, declaring Colonel Cresap's "De-
mand unreasonable; and the more so, as
no others complain of Injuries from those
Indians".

Some years later, in the Indian wars of
1763, an ineffectual attack was made, the
middle of July of that year, upon Cresap's
Fort. This is interestingly described in the
printed Cresap biography, written by one
of Colonel Cresap's own household, later

a Methodist minister, the Rev. John J. Jacob, he becoming the husband of the Colonel's widowed daughter-in-law. In this assaulting party, Jacob recounts, was Killbuck, an old Indian, who lay hidden, for three days under a bridge, that spanned the mill race close to the Fort, with the sole object of killing Cresap. In this, however, Killbuck was disappointed; he did not even see Cresap. To "add to his mortification", as he himself afterwards related, one day "an old [white] woman", unaware of the enemy beneath, "coming on the bridge, stopped directly over" his warriorship "and let her water upon him. Now, whether this old fellow had ever heard of the Philosopher Socrates and his wife Xantippe, I know not," continues Rev. Jacob, "but certain it is, that under similar circumstances he was more passive and silent than even Socrates himself."

Notwithstanding these occasional troubles with the Indians, Cresap, be it noted in passing, became a serviceable intermediary in the relations of the red men with the white men.

These Iroquois warriors are interestingly portrayed by yet another authoritative contemporary, Cadwallader Colden (1688–1776), Surveyor General of New York, in his *History of the Five Indian Nations* (London, 1747), pages 6–9, as follows:

"When any of the young Men of these Nations have a Mind to signalize themselves, and to gain a Reputation among their Countrymen, by some notable Enterprize against their Enemy, they at first communicate their Design to two or three of their most intimate Friends; and if they come into it, an Invitation is made, in their Names, to all the young Men of the Castle, to feast on Dog's Flesh; ...

"When the Company is met, the Promoters of the Enterprize set forth the Undertaking in the best Colours they can; they boast of what they intend to do, and incite others to join, from the Glory there is to be obtained; and all who eat of the Dog's Flesh, thereby inlist themselves.

"The Night before they set out, they make a grand Feast, to this all the noted Warriors of the Nation are invited; and here they have their War-Dance, to the Beat of a kind of Kettle-drum. The Warriors are seated in two Rows in the House, and each rises up in his Turn, and sings the great Acts he has himself performed, and the Deeds of his Ancestors; and this is always accompanied with a Kind of a Dance, ...; and from Time to Time, all present join in a Chorus, applauding every notable Act. ... I have sometimes persuaded some of their young Indians to act these Dances, for our Diversion ...

"They come to these Dances with their Faces painted in a frightful Manner, as they always are when they go to War, to make themselves terrible to their Enemies; and in this Manner the Night is spent. Next Day they march out with much Formality", in single file observing "a profound Silence".

Upon their departure "they always peel a large Piece of the Bark of some great Tree ... upon the smooth Side of this Wood they, with their red Paint, draw one or more Canoes going from Home, with the Number of Men in them padling, which go upon the Expedition; and some Animal, as a Deer or Fox, an Emblem of the Nation against which the Expedition is designed is painted at the Head of the Canoes; for they always travel in Canoes along the Rivers, which lead to the Country against which the Expedition is designed, as far as they can".

Upon their return "they represent on the same, or some Tree near it, the Event of the Enterprize, and now the Canoes are painted with their Heads turned towards the Castle; the Number of the Enemy killed, is represented by Scalps painted black, and the Number of Prisoners by as many Withs, (in their Painting not unlike Pothooks) with which they usually pinion their Captives. These Trees are the Annals, or rather Trophies of the Five Nations: I have seen many of them, and by them, and their War Songs, they preserve the History of their great Atchievements."

To revert, now, to the real hero of this piece. It was with one of these returning Iroquois bands, as depicted above in the pages of Colden and in the crude but realistic wording of Cresap and like immediate contemporaries, that the boy George Washington spent over a day and a half, while he was detained by the wet weather at Cresap's. In his Journal, under date of Wednesday, March 23rd, 1748, he gives this account of

AN IROQUOIS INDIAN DANCE

"Rain'd till about two oClock & Clear'd when we were agreeably Surpris'd at y^e. sight of thirty odd Indians coming from War with only one Scalp We had some Liquer with us of which we gave them Part it elevating there Spirits put them in y. Humeur of Dauncing of whom we had a War Daunce there Manner of Dauncing is as follows Viz They clear a Large Circle & make a Great Fire in y^e. middle then seats themselves around it y^e. Speaker makes a grand Speech telling them in what Manner they are to Daunce after he has finish'd y. best Dauncer Jumps up as one awaked out of a Sleep & Runs & Jumps about y. Ring in a most comicle

Wednesday 28th. Rain'd till about
two Oclock & Clear'd up when
we were agreeably surpris'd at ye
sight of thirty odd Indians coming
from War with only one Scalp. We
had some Liquor with us of which
we gave them Part it elevating there
Spirits put them in ye Humour of
Dauncing of whom we had a War
Daunce there manner of Daun
cing is as follows Viz. They clear
a Large Circle & make a great
Fire in ye middle then seats them
selves around it ye Speaker
makes a grand Speech

Description of the Indian Dance. Page of Washington's First Journal, in His Own Hand, Wednesday, March 28, 1748. Size 3¾ x 6 Inches

telling them in what manner they are to Dance after they have finished y.e best Dancer jumps up as one awaked out of a Sleep & runs & Jumps about y.e Ring in a most comicle Manner he is followed by y.e Rest then begins their Musicians to Play y.e Musick is a Pot half of Water with a Deer skin Streched over it as tight as it can & a Gourd with some shatt in it to Rattle & a Piece of an horses Tail tied to it to make y.e look fine y.e one keeps Ratteling and y.e other

Description of the Indian Dance. Page of Washington's First Journal, in His Own Hand. Continued

Manner he is followed by y^e. Rest then begins there Musicians to Play ye Musick is a Pot half [full] of Water with a Deerskin Stretched over it as tight as it can & a Goard with some Shott in it to Rattle & a Piece of an horses Tail tied to it to make it look fine y. one keeps Rattling and y. other Drumming all y^e. while y. others is Dauncing.

"Fryday 25th: 1748 nothing Remarkable on thursday but only being with y^e. Indians all day so shall slip it this day left Cresap's".[1]

His sojourn of three days with Thomas Cresap[2] as host, in such an enticing environment of frontiersmen and Indians, must have been a further extension of young George Washington's knowledge of men and manners. Like Ulysses he might

---

[1] Leaves 36 verso—35 verso.

[2] Of Washington's later visits to Cresap see Appendix, page 66.

well have said that he was a part of all that he had met. With the narrator apparently none the worse for his strenuous jaunt, but even better prepared for the hardships and perils to come, the narrative comes to an end, as follows:

"Wednesday ye 13th: of April 1748 M^r. Fairfax got safe home and I myself safe to my Brothers [at Mount Vernon] which concludes my Journal."[1]

---

[1] Leaf 29.

and after Riding about 20 Miles
we had 20 to go for we had lost
ourselves & got up as High as
Ashbys Bent we did get over
W[m]s Gap that Night and as
low as W[m] W[est]s in Fairfax
County 18 Miles from y[e] Top of
y[e] Ridge this day see a Rattle
ttel Snake y[e] first we had seen
in all our Journey

Wednesday y[e] 13th of April
1748

M[r] Fairfax got safe home and
Imyself safe to my Brothers

APPENDIX

GEORGE WASHINGTON'S ANCESTRY

[1] George Washington was of the fourth generation in this country, his father Augustine Washington, son of Lawrence Washington, by his wife, Mildred Warner, daughter of Augustine Warner, being the grandson of the immigrant, John Washington, by his wife, Ann Pope, daughter of Nathaniel Pope.

John Washington, who came over from his native England to Virginia, in 1656, was married there to Ann Pope. He sprang from a long line of good ancestry in England, as proved by the painstaking researches, over an extensive period, of Joseph Lemuel Chester, Henry F. Waters, H. Isham Longden, T. Pape, Charles Arthur Hoppin and like expert genealogists. Sulgrave Manor House, the home of his ancestors in England, is now preserved as a Washington Memorial. He was the eldest son of the Rev. Lawrence Washington (d. 1652), M.A., Fellow of Brasenose College, Oxford University, and Rector of Purleigh, County Essex, who was a son of Lawrence Washington, of Sulgrave Manor and Brington, County Northampton, by his wife, Margaret Butler, daughter of William Butler, of Tighes, County Sussex.

This latter Lawrence Washington was a son of Robert Washington, of Sulgrave, by his wife Elizabeth Light, daughter of Walter Light, of Radway, County Warwick. Robert Washington was a son of Lawrence Washington of Gray's Inn, London, Mayor of Northampton and the first Washington grantee of the Manor of Sulgrave, County Northampton, by his wife Anne Pargiter, daughter of Robert Pargiter, of Gretworth.

Mayor Lawrence Washington was a son of John Wash-

ington, of Warton, County Lancaster, by his wife Margaret
Kitson, daughter of Robert Kitson, of Warton. John Washington was a son of Robert Washington, of Warton, and grandson of Robert Washington, of Warton, County Lancaster, etc.

Rev. Lawrence Washington's wife, the mother of John
Washington, the Virginia immigrant, also came of families
of the County of Northampton. She was Amphilis Twigden
(1602–1655, buried at Tring), daughter of John Twigden
(buried at Spratton, 1611) of Littleton, Parish of Creaton
Parva, by his wife Ann Dyckons (buried at Tring, 1637),
daughter of William Dyckons, of Creaton Parva.

Mary Ball, the mother of George Washington, was a
daughter of Joseph Ball (1649–1711), of Epping Forest, Lancaster County, Virginia, by his wife Mary; and a grand-
daughter of William (c. 1615–1680) and Hannah Ball, who,
coming from England, about 1650, settled in Lancaster
County, on a plantation called "Millenbeck", on the Rappahannock River.

WASHINGTON'S
LATER VISITS TO THOMAS CRESAP

In his travels of later years George Washington made at
least four other visits to Colonel Cresap, as recorded in his
journals, printed in John C. Fitzpatrick, *Diaries of Washington* (4 volumes, Boston, Mass., 1925), as follows: on his
trip to Western Pennsylvania and Ohio, in 1770, on three
different occasions, at the age of 38; (1) October 8, "Vale[ntino]
Crawford joined us, and he and I went [26 miles] to Colo.
Cresap's leaving the Doctr [James Craik] at [Samuel] Prit-
chard's with my boy [negro slave] Billy [Lee],[1] who was taken
sick".—*Diaries*, I., pages 400–401. He went to "Colo. Cresap's,

---

[1] Purchased from Mary Lee, in 1768, for £68. 15s, serving
his master faithfully as body slave until freed by the latter's
will.

in ordr. to learn from him (being just arrivd from England) the particulars of the Grant said to be lately sold to Walpole and others, for a certain Tract of Country on the Ohio".— *Diaries*, I., page 405; (2) on the return journey, November, "Tuesday 27th. We got to Colo. Cresaps at the Old Town after calling at Fort Cumberland and breakfasting with one Mr. Innis at the New Store—opposite.—25 miles".—*Diaries*, I., page 449; (3) December 27, "Got to the Old Town to Colo. Cresap's, distant from Killam's [on George's Creek] about 25 Miles".—*Diaries*, I., page 452; (4) in 1784, September 8, when he was 52, "I again crossed the [Potomac] River and getting into the Waggon Road pursued my journey to the old Town where I overtook my Company and baggage— lodged at Colo. Cresaps." "9th ... was about to set out when it began to Rain ... rainy we remained here"

"10th Set off ... The Road from the Old Town to Fort Cumberland we found tolerably good," etc.—*Diaries*, II., pages 286–287.

INDEX

INDEX

73